REFLECTIONS

RIYA SIKKA

ISBN
Paperback: 979-8-89067-801-0
Hardcase: 979-8-89133-609-4

Dedication

To my parents,
For always loving and supporting me
And teaching me to be kind

My favourite quote
"Happiness can be found, even in the darkest of times, if one only
remembers to turn on the light."
—J.K. Rowling, Harry Potter and the Prisoner of Azkaban

A Collection of 41 poems that revolves around life,
relationships and self-introspection.

Contents

Contents

Contents

Reflections

Looking into the mirror, a flawless clean glass
Letting a quick figure pass
Do you see heartbreak, accusations, and jealousy?
Or happiness, smiles, and curiosity

Looking into clear waters, what do you realize?
Does it anger you or tranquilize?
Each painful salty tear drops to the surface
The ripple creates a serene chorus

Smiling into the mirror puts you at ease
A feeling that you immediately seize
As the water reflects us clearly
It gives us an amazing sense of serenity

Loss of Hope

As you walk down the dark hall
Tall shadows tower you along the wall
Strolling towards the long-forgotten desk
Strain and tension going through your chest

The minute lights are the only sign of glee
The whispers and sounds make you want to flee
You scream as you see the door shut
Petrified as you strut

The lights start to fade
You stay remote as the emotions invade
Each light diminishing is a loss of hope
Standing in the darkness shattered and broke

A Ghost

Floating around as a free spirit
Grieving as it ceases to exist
Watching everyone everyday
Trying to keep the sadness at bay

Every moment thinking of a loved one
Hating to see them glum
Malice to those who destroyed his every ounce
He has his blood boiling and wants to pounce

Hungry for revenge, driving him blind
So livid & thumping in his frozen mind
He doesn't want you to be like him
Be free and happy devoid of any mayhem

Blowing Out a Candle

The light diminishes and the darkness enters
Loneliness and exhaustion stir
As each flame dies away
You look at every door in the hallway

The smoke slithers in the air
Desperately finding the matches full of despair
Something appears behind you
Pale and still as a statue

Sprinting through the never-ending hall
Staying calm as you listen to the soft rainfall
Coming to a halt with a shocked choke
As you see the creature in the fading smoke

SAVE the PLANET
TROPICAL WORLD
NEW ZEALAND
Tauranga
J411

Climatic Change

Cutting down trees is very unfortunate
Climatic change is the outcome that humans create
It's like trees taking revenge by changing the weather
Climatic change links three things together

Cutting down trees is one humungous error
It destroys habitats and leave animals in terror
Reduction in oxygen levels is another huge impact
People have started suffering and that is a fact

Climatic changes have made living hard and chaotic
I wish the cure was in my pocket
Truly people will have to start acting fast
Or its repercussions would Everlast

Dandelion Story

A young lad picks up a mystical flower
While the clouds cry a midnight shower
He thinks of a wish in his mind
And the petals flew unassigned

He watches while the petals float out of sight
What happened next turned him white
Years passed he is not young anymore
His youth is gone, no friendships to restore

You don't know what he wished that night
The night where the petals took off without a fight
When I leave don't let anyone cry
As he left the dandelion only granted a lie

GOD SAID *to* MOSES,

"I AM
WHO
I AM."

EXODUS 3:14

I am Me

I am Me

I believe equality should be a reality

I want everyone to get this fact in their mentality

I dream about my future

I wish everything to be nurtured

I am Me

I feel the friendship with my friends

I believe love beyond galaxies transcend

I cry joyful tears of love and happiness

I believe everyone should know their worthiness

I am ME

We are worthy of keeping this planet safe

I am positive we are brave

I love everyone who is unique

I know everyone can succeed

Amnesia

Amnesia is not always in the mind

There can be memories that you don't want to find

It can be a memory of heartbreak, embarrassment, or anguish

Any memory that you would not want to cherish

A memory that forever keeps you scarred

These reminders can only dwell in the heart

But the mind can protect you from getting hurt

Stop you from being thrown around like dirt

Sometimes the mind can be the foe

Allowing the memories to follow

Permitting despair and jealousy break you

Forcing you to think you're the issue

G07
ARES
HAVEN
HELL

Heaven

Two children playing calmly on a cliff
Little do they know what is going to occur is not a bliss
Both fall in the depths of hell
But God won't let them stay there to dwell

They both get sent to heaven away from the Devil
They float up to the highest level
The children are happier than ever
As God opened the gates to enter

They saw everyone sad down on Earth
So, they turned death into a wish instead of a curse
They made their wish quite worthwhile
When one looks up, they don't cry but smile

Whispers

Voices running through your head
Letting the chills and horror spread
Listening to every murmur that you can catch
Then you realize and light up like a match

You think carefully where you have heard this
As you ponder and try to focus
You suddenly recall these phrases
And your mind flashes faces

They are faces of your loved ones
Who made your smile worth a thousand sun's
Quickly you remember, they are gone
When they leave, there is an empty zone

Tomorrow

Dreading the next day
Wanting to live forever in today
Tomorrow can be a fresh start
When you can erase each mark

Each step brings you closer to the future
All special moments that you can capture
This is a time to wipe all tears
A time to face all fears

Never be afraid of tomorrow
As you never know of all the wonders that follow
Have courage and fight through the panic
Time will fly like magic

CAN
CAN
CAN
CAN

Fichet-Bauche   GUNNEBO
902 234 235

A Second

Every passing second is a miracle
Moments when we chuckle,
Moments when we cry,
Moments when we sigh,

Moments when we had queries and doubts
Those moments always count
Embrace every second of the day
Don't just flick it away

Life is something we should value
Even if we feel dismayed and Blue
Some seconds are stuck in strife
Think positive, cause that's life

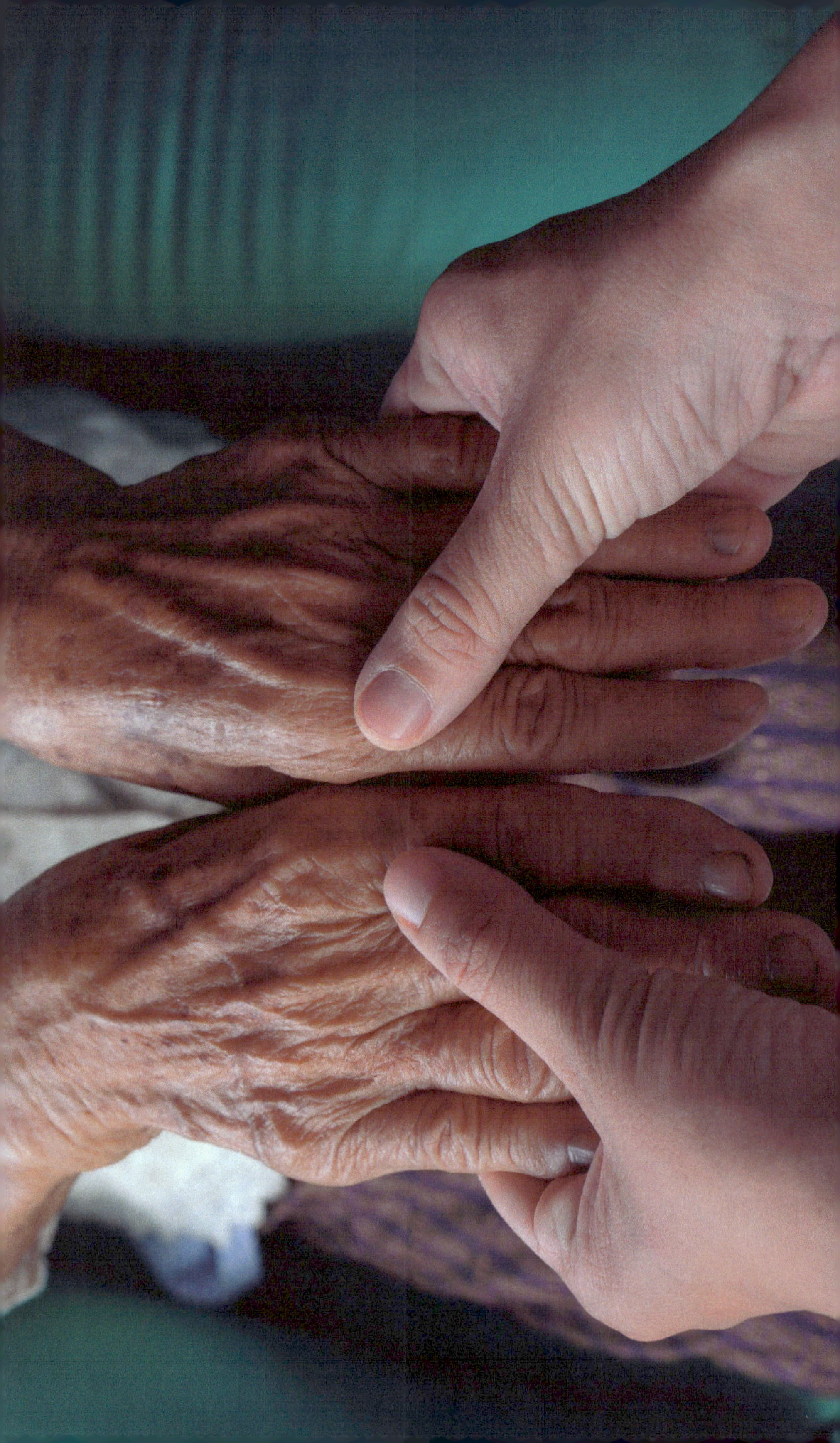

Grandma

Cooks the best nourishing food
Always tries to change your mood
Always guides you what is the best for you
Supports you on what you want to pursue

Love you to the moon and back
Honesty and love is something they will never lack
Whatever comes from them is always true
With them around you never feel blue

They look at you with pride in their face
Believe in whatever you do, you will be an ace
Their smile lights up your whole world
The pain in you makes them concerned

Home

A Home is always a safe place
Memories are built that no one can erase
In a home love and dreams never end
It's a place where everything mends

In your home, dreams become a reality
A home is filled with loyalty and honesty
In a home you are always filled with glee
The concept is always WE never ME

A home is the first place when you open your eyes
Where you had your first cries
Every home has a mantra
It's where the tooth fairy comes along with Santa

Hug

A Hug makes you feel safe and secure
Feeling sad! A warm hug is the perfect cure
A Hug makes all those tears disappear
Back from a holiday a hug is the best souvenir

When you are in an embrace your mind clears up
When you are alone, a hug is the best pick up
A hug gives you much happiness and relief
A hug will erase all your grief

A warm feel keeps all dangers far away
To the land of happiness, a cuddle is a passageway
Once you get wrapped in a bear hug
You will forever be snug

Mum

Without you I wouldn't exist
Love everything about you, it's an endless list
There is always room in my heart for you
With you around I am never blue

When I lay my eyes on you, I burst with joy
My love for you is something I will never destroy
Thank you for always being with me
Always opening my eyes to something new to see

Thank you for removing all obstacles out of my way
For me you are like the morning's first ray
Thank you for protecting me from whatever may come
That's why I am proud to say you are my mum

Sunrise

Delaying each moment in the present
Not knowing that tomorrow isn't fluorescent
Preoccupied in something less dear
Ignoring the people, you share each tear

By then it's too late
As the mistake is quite great
Regretting your thoughtless efforts
You could have prevented these murk's

Thinking of times with the loved ones
And all that could have been done
Don't delay and be full of sorrows
You don't know will the sun rise tomorrow

On the Way to School

I am sprinting like in a race
Sweat is running down my face
I can visualize going to detention in my mind
I highly doubt if my teacher will be kind

Sweating I look like a blurry haze
Everything is numb as I am in a horrified daze
Scared I will not see the end of this day
Good luck is what I need someone to say

Rushing past everyone that's in my way
Heart beating rapidly, trying to keep my panic at bay
Finally reaching my school
Praying my teacher won't be too cruel

Parents

The moment they lay eyes on you
Their love for you is unconditional and true
Each year seeing you grow is a marvel
Their love for you is never partial

Health and happiness is all they wish for you
Whatever you desire they will make it come true
They show appreciation with a genuine heart
Their love and adoration is off the chart

Their mind strength is amazing to believe
All they want for you is to succeed
Their love for you will never disappear
Make sure you always keep them near

Winter

Some loathe this season
Some love it for no reason
Drinking hot chocolate every day
Throwing snowballs is fun, they say

"Swish!" "Plop" the snowballs say
They are cold but as soft as clay
Prancing around in the rain
You don't feel sane

As Spring draws closer
Weather starts to feel warmer
Some are disappointed this is the end of winter
Some are getting ready for spring then Summer

Sunshine

Sunshine lights up the world with joy and love
It comes from the loved ones above
Gets you up and going everyday
It shines up your heart instead of feeling grey

Sun shines in everyone
It brings out the glory and fun
Brightness inside you changes your world
Your love for loved ones will always be reserved

In the darkness, sunshine finds a way inside
Keeps you ecstatic and puts worries aside
Sunshine overpowers anything that is delusional
When it shines on you, you always feel special

Petunia

As petunia grows into your heart
Crack by crack it makes you fall apart
Both pieces are pitch black
Overtaken by rage you feel like getting a cardiac

It spreads quickly, overpowering your wisdom
Jealousy, and rage ruins your system
Tears start swelling up your eyes
Infront of others, you put on a disguise

Angry and your energy at zero percent
Everything around you makes you overwhelmed
The thoughts inside make you gloomier
All these emotions turn you moodier

A Tree

How can one tree bring in so many memories?
Dreams, happiness, tears are all it screams
Each branch, each leaf holds a memory
Each twig and mass is like a treasury

When you climb, each step brings a smile
Bringing back memories, makes you feel alive
People are not always the solution to a problem
A tree can heal from being solemn

There is a tree of life for a reason
It nurtures you with love without question
Memories are engraved deep in every shrub
Full of tears, smiles, pride, laughs and cuts

Christmas

This Holiday is always a blast
I wish it would go slower than fast
Christmas brings happiness and joy
This holiday isn't about receiving a toy

It's about family and love
A bird symbolising Christmas is a beautiful dove
This holiday gives you a tranquil soul
Make sure you are at the top of Santa's roll

Christmas always keep you merry
A fruit representing Christmas, is a sweet cherry
Christmas keeps your heart shining bright
Gifts, cookies, and love makes a beautiful sight

Fog

As you walk into the murky mist
It's hard to think this beauty can exist
Waking up in the morning
Looking at the clouds start to be forming

Rapidly you get ready for the day
There is no sun out to your dismay
Instead, the sight is quite unusual
It is unique and amazingly beautiful

The air is full of murk
When you move forward behind it lurks
Its sauntering into a big bubble
The beauty is truly incredible

Moonlight

As you step into the shadows of the trees
Your hair sways along with the breeze
You run through the smearing fog
Jumping joyfully above each log

The shining moon illuminates the whole topiary
Running through the leaves is quite merry
Strolling just to relax
Going astray within your tracks

The trees hovering around like a protector
Allowing your mind to go on an adventure
The sky is a mix of white and grey
Gives one a feeling of being happy and gay

Gracefully

Gracefully the bird flies in the Breeze
Gracefully she lands on a thin long branch
Gracefully she sings to her newborn babies
Gracefully they flap their wings for the first time

Gracefully they copy their mother
Gracefully they take off into the Breeze
Gracefully they grow to young adult birds
Gracefully they partner with another bird

Gracefully together they find a new home
Gracefully they love one another to a great extent
Gracefully they have adorable chicks
Gracefully they take off into the Breeze

Wish

Holidays

Holidays are filled with joy
It's a feeling that you enjoy
It is about spending time with loved ones
Gives you happiness the size of many suns

Happiness and glee takes over your mind
Allows you to take a moment to rewind
You can feel the cheerfulness in the air
Everyone showing love and care

Joy is everywhere where you walk
Strolling as you get lost in thought
Laughs and smiles is displayed on every face
Grins becoming contagious as you pace

enjoy
the
little
things

Life

In Life you will get nightmares and dreams
Sometimes life will not be what it may seem
Life's plans can change in a flash
But stay optimistic and let is all crash

Friends and Family always stick by your side
With them there is no reason to hide
You may feel there is no hope left
All you must do is sit down and reflect

Each night is part of this journey
Never think this moment is not worthy
Cherish each time, don't let it go to waste
It won't come back even in a haste

The Snowman

A young girl playing in the freezing snow
As the wind rushes past with a strong blow
Building up each snowman inch by inch
Bits of ice hit her, but she didn't flinch

It's a piece of two people with a grin
Identical, smiling like a twin
Suddenly the girl sobs
Her tears are as soft as the raindrops

She runs inside to her mother
Surprised the mother goes to the structure
She goes pale and her heart pumps faster
As the snowman looks like the girl's father

Ballerina's Story

A young girl sees a dream
Wishing to be a Ballerina; dancing makes her gleam
Next day she gets a tutu and ballet shoes
Dancing till she left her youth

She believed she had outgrown her dance
Left without a second glance
She took on housework
Got exhausted and went berserk

She wanted to return to her dream
But it wasn't as easy as it would seem
She developed a serious injury in her knee
Making her quit before completing the journey

The Suffocating Vines

Wandering through the long vines
Your face distracted and bleak in the moonshine
Feeling the vines wrapped around you
Ignore as you don't have a clue

It slithers down your neck
Starting to build up sweat
It gets tighter and tighter
Each second making you whiter

Desperately trying to wriggle out
Writhe and hopelessly try to shout
Eyes shut and your heart starts to pound
Gradually you drop to the ground

Death

As we stand outside the care ward
Seeing a loved one hanging to its last chord
Crying as you hope for the best
Sitting tight as the doctors run the tests

With the rest of the family beside you
Contemplating all the that you could undo
Suddenly you hear a beep cut off
Horrified that is their last cough

Realization finally dawns on you
Knowing the end of their chapter is due
Again, breaking down in weeps
Hoping they have a tranquil long sleep

Hope

In Life there will be ups and downs
Keep your head high with no frowns
Sometimes you feel there is no Hope
And your life is going down like a slope

Remember never lose faith
It makes sure you are safe
Fate and confidence solves it all
Keep your hopes high and take a freefall

Sometimes life depends on only hope
Saves you when you feel remote
Sometimes the mind lays out negative thoughts
Ignore and go for a soothing walk

Space

As each star glows in the mysterious night
It raises a twinkle in your eye, nice and bright
The Milky way stretches to a distance
The sun has its own brilliance

No one knows what lies beyond the Milky way
It would be fun to float and go astray
Saturn, Mercury, and Mars are just a few planets
It's amazing to feel the universe wrap you like a blanket

Skimming rings around the Saturn
Each star as bright as lanterns
The moon floats in silence
All the planets are in best alliance

Dawn

In the darkness you sleep and rest
As your breath slows in your chest
There is a faint glow in the sky
Watching over you far too high

Deep in thoughts as you lay still
Nightmares send your body a strong shrill
As dawn gets closer every minute
The stars fade away like a lonely spirit

Who knows what happens in the next moment
This time of the dawn feels very pleasant
It's a shame this time shall come to an end
As your consciousness begins to ascend

I am Sorry

I am sorry for the innocence we stole

I am sorry for treating you like plain coal

I am sorry for ignoring the screams and tears

I am sorry for not caring about your heart that has sears

I am sorry for not seeing your tears of sadness

I am sorry for not thinking to stop this madness

I am sorry for putting your traditions to an end

I am sorry for the inequality that is yet to mend

I am sorry that we ostracize you by your skin

I am sorry that we killed you from within

I am sorry for stealing the prosperity

I am sorry for leading you to adversity

Fear

Running right through the forest
Believing this is happening is the hardest
Your fears coming true through a nightmare
Your heart beating faster with a scare

You want to get over these horrific fears
While your face is smeared with tears
You feel your eye pushing through the seam
That's when you know it's all a dream

Your entire body gushes with relief
The amount of time it lasts is quite brief
Then you see something that fills you with horror
Someone standing in the corner

Day into Night

As the sun rises above the foamy clouds
Morning gets filled with birds and beautiful sounds
The day looks stunning and bright
Comes the noon, time starts running out of sight

This time of the day is when the sun has an effect
A time for you to ponder and reflect
As noon starts to merge into eve
It's the time you can settle down and relieve

The sky turns to a shade of orange, purple and blue
Swiftly turns into a pitch black view
Close your eyes and doze away!
Until the sun shines its first ray

(KEEP A
BREAST)

Tattoo

Drop by Drop the ink engraves in the skin
Allowing the pigment to spin
Eventually it forms a picture
But the meaning is so much bigger

Tears well up from memory
Being thankful you are over the horrific journey
Now that you have the mind strength
To finish everything at length

The image made of ink comes to an end
So is the painful time something to fend
This time is no longer solemn
The tattoo is a semicolon

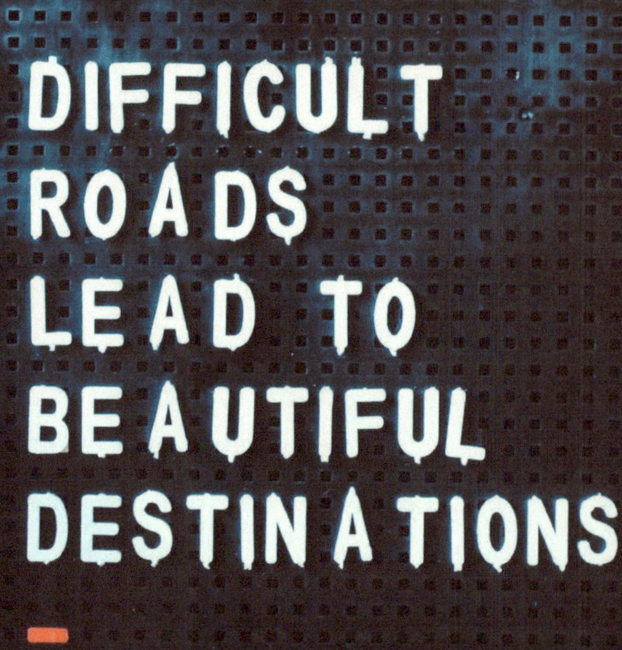

DIFFICULT
ROADS
LEAD TO
BEAUTIFUL
DESTINATIONS

Success

Reaching the pinnacle of success is heaven
It also means you are due for a lesson
There is one thing that can give you success
FAILURE can alone help you commence

Failure pushes you to work harder
Gives you the power to conquer
It may feel like a punishment or a warning
Haunting you when you wake up in the morning

All you need is to push towards your goal
Put your entire Heart and soul
That's the only way to progress
Climbing the ladder of success

About the Author

Riya a Grade 6 student resides in Melbourne with her parents. She is an avid reader along with having a love for literature.

Her sentiments and deep feeling for the real-world situations symbolises in her poetry. Riya's work makes the reader echo on their inner self.

Making a splash as a new author she was nominated for the "Young Achiever Award "by Channel 7- a prominent Australian television network. She has also been bestowed with the "Global kids achiever award" after the publication of her first book.

Poetry is like nurturing a flower
It yields a lot of power
If you water, it grows day by day
But if you give up, it will decay

— By Riya Sikka